THE
MIGHTY
MEKONG

Course of the Mekong River

Thanglha Mountains
TIBET   Kham Region
Yangtze R.
Yüshu
Mekong
Chamdo
HIMALAYAS
Salween R.
Lhasa
River
CHINA
Yangtze R.
Chungking
Brahmaputra R.
INDIA
Mekong
Paoshan
Kunming
Irrawaddy R.
Canton
BURMA
River
Salween R.
North
Hanoi
20°   20°
Nam Seng
Luang
Prabang   Hainan I.
Pak Lay
L A O S
Vientiane
Mekong River
15°   Gulf of   Nam Savannakhet   SOUTH   15°
Martaban   Chao   Pong R.
Phraya   T H A I L A N D
V I E T N A M
Angkor Thom   Khong   Khone Falls
CAMBODIA   CHINA
Tonle
Sap L.   Kratie   South
Hau Giang
10°   Phnom Penh   Saigon   10°
Bassac R.   SEA

0   100   200   300
Miles

Drawn by Miklos Pinther
MALAYA
5°   100°   105°   110°   5°

THE
MIGHTY
MEKONG

by Howard Liss

illustrated with photographs

Hawthorn Books, Inc.
Publishers   New York

THE MIGHTY MEKONG

First Edition: 1967

5950

1439332

For my daughters
Jodi Robin
and
Dana Jennifer

"Learn about other countries.
It will help you to understand your own."

ACKNOWLEDGMENTS

The author wishes to thank the following individuals and institutions, without whose invaluable assistance this book could not have been written:

Mr. Khamchan Pradith, Counsellor of Embassy, Permanent Mission of Laos to the United Nations.

Mr. Nathaniel O. Abelson, Curator, the United Nations Map Room.

Mr. Shish-Kang Tung, Curator, the Gest Oriental Library and Far Eastern Collections, Princeton University, and his assistant, Mrs. Lucy Loh.

Dr. James C. Cain, Mayo Clinic, personal medical representative of the President of the United States to Saigon, South Vietnam.

The staffs of the United Nations Photo Collection; the New York Public Library; the American Geographical Society; the Permanent Missions to the United Nations of Laos and Tibet.

The author also wishes to thank Mr. Khamchan Pradith for permission to use his poem "Life in a Lao Village."

Contents

1   The Course of the Mekong River   13

2   The Upper Mekong in Tibet   18

3   The Mekong in China and Burma   37

4   The Mekong in Laos and Thailand   52

5   The Mekong in Cambodia   74

6   The Mekong in South Vietnam   88

7   The Future of the Mekong   102

    Bibliography   107

    Index   109

THE
MIGHTY
MEKONG

CHAPTER 1

The Course of the Mekong River

High in the forbidding Himalaya Mountains of Tibet, amid the vast snow fields and glaciers of the plateaus, many of the great rivers of Asia are born: the Yellow and Yangtze rivers of China, the Irrawaddy and Salween rivers of Burma, and the Brahmaputra River of India. Some 16,400 feet above sea level, in the Tangin Pass, a number of small swift streams are formed out of the melting glacial ice. As they rush down the heights to join together, they become the headwaters of yet another river. In Tibet it is called the Nam Chu or Dzachu. To the Chinese it is the Lants'ang Kiang—the "turbulent river." This is the Mekong, eleventh longest river in the world, which helps to shape the lives and destinies of more than fifty million Asian people.

The Mekong has been called "the Great International River." It begins its winding 2,600-mile course in eastern Tibet, with few tributaries adding to its cascading torrents during the first 750 miles. For most of this distance it runs parallel to two other mighty rivers, the Salween to the west and the Yangtze to the east. In some places the three river valleys are only twenty miles apart, separated by towering mountain ranges, some of whose peaks rise to heights of 15,000 feet. As the Mekong tumbles across the rugged terrain of Sikang and Yünnan provinces of China, some small tributaries add their waters. There are mountains here, too, but they are not as high, as bleak and forbidding as they were farther north. The countryside is greener and more picturesque. A few small villages appear, although not many of these are along the banks of the river.

Twisting and turning its way out of China, the Mekong becomes a marked border between Laos and Burma for some 130 miles. Then, suddenly, the same river, flowing along its erratic course, is the frontier between Laos and Thailand for a 62-mile stretch.

As though weary of being a national boundary, the Mekong swings into Laos. There it follows a rapids-filled course through a desolate area of forests and mountains, where additional streams race into the valley to join the parent river.

It is now that changes begin, not so much in the Mekong River as in the inhabitants of its banks. Where once there were only leopards, tigers, elephants, cobras and lizards, now there are signs of people, first in tiny hamlets, then in larger villages. Finally the Mekong flows in triumph through its first major city, the royal Laotian capital, Luang Prabang. Now its surface is covered with huge teak logs floating to market, and with sampans and pirogues, the small river boats of Asia.

Aerial view of the Mekong river. *(Courtesy of the Shell Oil Co.)*

From this point the Mekong reverses its direction, arcing to the south and then east, and after a 373-mile journey through Laos only, once more it becomes the frontier between Laos and Thailand. Still on a meandering course, the great river passes through the Laotian administrative capital, Vientiane, and then south into the town of Savannakhet. Beyond this populated center the character of the Mekong changes again. It becomes a raging torrent of rapids and rocky gorges as additional tributaries rush in to add to the thunder of the waters. The chief hazard to river travel is the Khone Falls, which drop seventy-two feet within six and a quarter miles.

Through the rest of Laos and into Cambodia flows the Mekong, to keep a rendezvous later with rivers that are somewhat larger than before, such as the Nam Seng, the Se Noi, and others.

It is in central Cambodia that the Mekong makes its presence and power felt the most, especially during the monsoon season, from early May through late September.

In central Cambodia lies a large body of water, the Tonle Sap, which in Cambodian means "Great Lake." The lake flows out through a river which bears the same name. The Tonle Sap River joins the Mekong at the Cambodian capital, Phnom Penh. As the torrential monsoon rains pour into the Mekong, it overflows its banks with such ferocity that the Tonle Sap River actually backs up, reverses its course and flows back into the great Tonle Sap Lake again, tripling its size and sometimes more, depending on the amount of rainfall. Later, when the rains stop and the flood waters ebb, the people living around the Tonle Sap Lake harvest millions of tons of fish, to be canned, salted, smoked, or sold fresh in the market places.

Now the Mekong begins its final long run to the delta region. Crossing the Cambodian border into South Vietnam, it throws off a river here and there, the chief of these being the Hau Giang, to go its own way.

Densely populated settlements line the banks of the Mekong during these final miles. Here is the "rice bowl" of Asia, with the Mekong furnishing the water for the endless paddies. Here also, in the swampy lowlands of the delta, is the center of a tragedy, of people torn by civil strife.

Running through the delta, the Mekong and its tributaries are connected by smaller streams and man-made canals, which provide irrigation and help in the drainage of swamps. The mouths of the streams have shifting mudbanks which build up very rapidly because of sedimentation.

At last the journey is ended. As though weary of its long run through mountains, rapids, and swamp country, the Mekong flows out of South Vietnam and gives up its waters to the South China Sea.

CHAPTER 2

The Upper Mekong
in Tibet

In eastern Tibet, in the Kham region, four of Asia's greatest rivers have their headwaters: the Brahmaputra, Salween, Mekong, and Yangtze. They are formed from rivulets trickling out of the constantly snow-capped mountains and glaciers that sprawl over most of the country. The Brahmaputra drops away toward India to the west, but the Salween, Mekong, and Yangtze form almost parallel lines as they flow south. Sometimes they are a mere twenty miles apart, but in a way each is in a different world, for they are separated by towering mountain peaks, some of them rising to heights of more than 15,000 feet. The Nu Shan ("Shan" means "mountain range" in Chinese) divides the Mekong from the Salween to the west, while the Yünling Shan separates the Mekong from the Yangtze to the east.

It was the French explorer Dutreuil de Rhins who discovered and mapped the headwaters of the Mekong. De Rhins was later

Tibet's Himalayan Mountains. *(Office of Tibet)*

murdered in Tibet, but not before he had overcome great hardships, fighting the winds, the weather, and terrain across the barren wastes of eastern Tibet. He pinpointed the source of the powerful river in the Tangin Pass of the Thanglha Mountains, 16,400 feet above sea level, at approximately 32 degrees north latitude, 95 degrees east longitude.

Much of the later exploration of the Mekong was done by French missionaries and by British botanists, such as Frank Kingdon Ward, who searched for new species of plants in the wilds of Tibet. The task was dangerous, not only because of the forbidding land but also because some of the Tibetan lamas resented the presence of the missionaries. In 1905 they banded together and killed every missionary they could find in the Mekong valley.

Travelers seldom venture into this part of the world, especially those from the western hemisphere. In 1950 the Chinese invaded Tibet and gained control of the country, making it a province of China. In 1958 the Tibetans tried to free themselves from Chinese domination, but the revolt failed. The Dalai Lama, who is the spiritual leader of Tibet, was forced to flee into India by a secret route. The Chinese installed another religious official in his place, the Panchen Lama, who was more friendly toward them. Today, travel is stopped and only those people who are approved by the Chinese government can venture into Tibet.

There is another reason for the lack of visitors into eastern Tibet. To reach the region near the Mekong would require weeks of trekking across steep ranges, through mountain passes, over sketchy trails that suddenly disappear into trackless country. It would be necessary to secure the services of porters and guides who are familiar with the region. All equipment and rations would have to be carried on the backs of mules and tough mountain ponies. In the winter, these animals could not get through the deep snows, and yaks—powerful, hairy oxen—would be needed. Even for these strong creatures passage through deep snow drifts would be difficult. However, the yak drovers have perfected a system that works. The lead animal lunges ahead through the high drifts, clearing a path through the snow until it is tired and can no longer move forward. Then it lies down and the next yak in line moves ahead, passing the first one, clearing a further path until it too is tired and lies down. Another yak follows, and the procedure is carried out until all the animals have reached solid ground, out of the deep snow drifts.

The Dalai Lama. *(Office of Tibet)*

Another travel hazard is the thin air. At altitudes of 14,000 to 15,000 feet, outsiders would have difficulty breathing in the rarefied atmosphere. Only the Tibetans, who are used to it, can live there.

But suppose we could take a trip down the Mekong, from its source to its mouth. It would be a long, difficult journey, with great danger from wild animals, the elements, and disease. For more than 1,000 miles there would be few people living along the banks of the river. There is no record of any man who has ever *attempted* such a trip, let alone completed it successfully. But many men have traced a route along the Mekong one section at a time. Perhaps, by putting all the sections together, it will be possible to make that 2,600-mile journey.

As the streams sluice out of the rocky crags and onto the flat plateau, they converge to form a river bed. Here at the headwaters the Mekong is wide but still shallow and can be forded by simply wading across. An occasional isolated *gomba*, which is the Tibetan word for monastery, can be found, but there are very few inhabited villages.

As the newborn river continues southward, other streams join it. With the additional water rushing it along, the Mekong courses out of the plateaus and begins a roaring run through steep ravines and rocky gorges. Navigation at this point and for hundreds of miles to come is impossible. Any boat caught in the powerful currents would be smashed to splinters against the rocks jutting out of the river bed or along the banks.

There are no people living by the Mekong's banks in Tibet. The sheer cliffs and the steeply sloping embankments make it impossible even to pitch a tent. And there is great danger of serious illness from the swarms of malarial mosquitoes infesting the river valley. It may seem strange to discover malaria at altitudes of more than 12,000 feet, but in summer the temperatures in the Mekong gorges climb quite high. During July, the humidity, caused by air currents trapped inside the ravines and sprays of water hurled from the rapids, makes the valley an ideal breeding ground for mosquitoes.

However, it is because of the heat and humidity that there is a great variety of plant life along the banks of the Mekong. Vast fields of yellow meadow flowers and red dwarf rhododendrons cover the steep slopes and the flatter land beyond. There are huge forests of pine and juniper—the latter called "scented wood trees" by the Tibetans. Butterflies go winging through the forests. The ground seems to be alive with millions of pesty sand fleas.

It is only some distance away from any of the three rivers— Salween, Mekong, or Yangtze—that any village is to be found. Such a hamlet might consist of a clump of twenty-five or thirty houses, with dark, narrow lanes running between them, jammed together into the side of a hill. The villages are widely scattered, isolated from each other by the mountains. They are not to be found on an ordinary map. In fact a large part of Tibet is still unmapped, unexplored.

Villagers or travelers wishing to cross the Mekong in this part of the headwater region can do so only by using a kind of "sling-and-rope" device. The ropes, made of twisted canebrake or bamboo, are securely fastened to a high place on one bank and a low spot on the other. The slings are made of hollowed-out wood or sometimes yak hides. The person (or animal) crossing the river is fastened inside the sling, which has one end looped around the rope, and then the sling slides down the rope and across the river. The crossing is made at terrific speed, sling and passenger skimming perilously close to the swirling waters of the Mekong. Because of the tremendous friction of sling against rope, the twisted strands of canebrake must be constantly greased with layers of yak butter. The slide down the rope is so fast that sometimes, when the grease has begun to wear away, the friction causes the rope to burn. Naturally, the ropes do not last long. At best they must be replaced every three months, although they do not last that long when river-crossing traffic is heavy.

The Mekong surges along its turbulent course, through deep gullies and gorges for perhaps 200 miles before it reaches a town of some size. This is Chamdo (the Chinese have changed its name to Ch'angtu), the chief town of the Kham region, built on the heights near the Mekong gorge.

Since ancient times there has been a caravan route, starting in the northern town of Jyekundo (now Yüshu), moving south through Chamdo, then southwest for some 370 miles to the city of Lhasa, capital of Tibet. Chinese merchants sent out shipments of silk, satin, brocades, cotton goods, and tea, which was pressed into the shape of bricks for convenience. Chamdo became a thriving commercial center as the drovers and their caravans of mules and camels used the town as a stopover, later crossing the Mekong over a sturdy suspension bridge and continuing the long journey. Few such caravans make that trip today, and those that do are loaded mostly with musk and medicinal herbs. There are a number

Lhasa, the capital of Tibet. *(Office of Tibet)*

of shops left in Chamdo but not much in the way of goods. Yet, because there are no other towns of comparable size in the area, it is still considered the commercial center of the Kham region.

Chamdo is sometimes called the "city of lamaseries." Beautiful old temples, some of them centuries old, are scattered through the town. But they have suffered damage and are in disrepair. Constant battles against invading Chinese troops and marauding bandits—the danger of mountain bandits exists even today—have chipped away at the buildings, and as far as is known they have not been rebuilt to any great extent.

The lama temples of Tibet began to be built some time during the eighth century. A Buddhist monk named Padmasambhava (his name means "born of the lotus") journeyed into Tibet from northern India. The Tibetans of that time practiced a religion that was really a form of nature worship. Padmasambhava established his form of Buddhism, a religion that came to be called Lamaism. It is a great deal like the Buddhism of China and other Asian countries, except that Lamaism also contains parts of the Hindu religion. The early followers of Padmasambhava spread his teaching throughout Tibet. Today there is no village or hamlet that does not have a temple, or lamasery, and some are found in the wilderness, where there is no village for miles around. According to some estimates there are only 1,300,000 people in all of Tibet, and about 500,000 of them are lamas, or monks.

Lamas worship in their temples three times a day. The tolling of a bell calls them into the lamasery, and they are seated in rows according to rank. Accompanied by the music of horns, drums, or trumpets they chant their hymns, using types of rosaries, as well as prayer wheels and prayer flags, charms and talismans. On special holidays or festivals, such as the New Year (which begins in February for them and means the beginning of spring), the lamaseries are decorated. Worshippers bring offerings of tea, flour, milk, and yak butter. Other religious holidays include the Flower Feast in summer, commemorating the birth of Buddha, and the Water Feast in August and September, which denotes the beginning of autumn.

Tibetans are among the most religious people in the world. They also cling to a great many superstitions. The people have faith in the power of charms and amulets and carry around boxfuls to protect themselves from the evil spirits that live in caves. Many of the charms are beautiful. In parts of Tibet, including the Mekong

Tibetans celebrate religious holiday. (*Office of Tibet*)

headwater region, the people make charms and amulets to sell, and a few are exported.

Most ancient countries have their share of legends and myths, and Tibet is no exception. One such legend deals with their ancestors and how they came to live in this land. Many, many centuries ago, "Po," as the natives call Tibet, was simply one huge lake. The water covered even the highest peak of their soaring mountain ranges. The Manushin Buddha, whose name was Amithaba, cut through the Himalayas, making channels to the southwest, and all the waters drained away. Now the land was dry, but there were still no people. So the "Lord of Mercy" came in the shape of a monkey. In the mountains he met a "she-devil" and married her. Six children were born of the marriage, but all of them looked like monkeys. The father fed the children sacred grain and soon the hair on their bodies disappeared. Their tails grew shorter and shorter and at last dropped off. These six children are the ancestors of the Tibetan people. Those who took after their father were intelligent and full of faith, love, and piety. They were eloquent and humble. Those who followed their mother's character were sinful and jealous, greedy and mischievous. But all six children were brave and strong, and so are all Tibetans today.

There are no mechanized industries in Tibet. The people have only two basic occupations: agriculture and raising animals. The herds consist of yaks, some sheep, perhaps a few goats, horses, and sometimes camels. The yaks are the most important domestic animals in Tibet. Farmers use the powerful beasts as work animals, to carry heavy loads and drag a plow across the hard ground. Everybody in Tibet eats yak meat, drinks yak milk, eats yak butter, and uses the hair and hides for shelter.

Many of the herdsmen (called *drok-pa* in Tibetan) are nomads, driving their animals from place to place in search of forage grasses. The Kham region, through which the Mekong flows, is the greenest in Tibet, so that it is comparatively easy to raise herds in that area, easier at any rate than in most other parts of the barren, mountainous land.

If we were to meet a Tibetan herdsman along the Mekong route, we would probably find him friendly and hospitable. In greeting he would lift up his hands to show that he has no weapons, stick out his tongue and point upward with his thumbs.

The large tent in which he and his family live is made of the woven hair and hide of yaks. After pitching his tent, the herdsman

Tibetan nomads with their animals. *(Office of Tibet)*

Herdsmen making tea. *(Office of Tibet)*

cuts blocks of hard turf and stacks them inside the shelter for protection against the cold cutting winds that howl through the mountains. These stacks of turf also serve as a sort of shelf for his meager household goods: a teapot made of iron or clay and some cooking and eating pans. The stove is made of mud or stones and yak-dung is the chief fuel. Dung gives off a terrible odor, but Tibetans are used to it.

Undoubtedly the herdsman would offer us some tea. Everybody in Tibet drinks huge quantities of tea, far more than the English or Chinese. About thirty or forty cups a day is average, for to them it is more a food than a beverage. To prepare their tea, they first tear a handful of leaves from a brick of tea and put it into a kettle of cold water. A bit of soda ash is added and the mixture brought to a boil. The hot liquid is then poured into a churn and is mixed together with some salt and a lump of yak butter as large as a man's fist. The tea is poured into earthenware or copper vessels and served. It looks more like soup than tea, but for Tibetans it is warming and nourishing.

Later, we would go outside to look at his herd which might consist of yaks and one or two horses. Off in the distance we might see wild animals grazing: mule deer, wild goats, and asses. Such game is surprisingly plentiful in the province but difficult to bag. That is where the herdsman's dog is used. Tibetan dogs are fast, well trained, and make excellent hunters. If the herdsman is lucky, his dog can surprise a deer, run it down, and trap it so that the herdsman can kill it. When that happens, there is a welcome change in the family diet.

Otherwise, the food is almost always the same—yak meat, cheese,

Nomads carry salt to trade for grain. (*Office of Tibet*)

and butter. Yak butter is one of the staples in the diet of all Tibetans. It is used for cooking and as a fuel for lamps. It is also important for rubbing on the faces and bodies of small children to protect them against the winter's cold. The butter is shaped into images and decorations for the lamaseries. In some instances butter is used as money to pay for other things.

Because they travel so much with their herds, most nomads have little opportunity to get flour or vegetables, unless they can make a trade with a farmer. Then they might get some corn, or flour made of roasted barley. The flour will be mixed with a little water to make a ball of dough and eaten without baking. Another scarce commodity for many Tibetans is salt. The people of the Kham region do have some, but west of the Mekong traders have to barter for it, exchanging corn for salt.

Herdsmen must be constantly on the alert for dangerous animals. Roaming the uplands of the Mekong are wolves, leopards, and sloth bears. If a herdsman doesn't have a gun, he protects himself with a slingshot made of horsehair and wool. And he is a deadly shot. With a good-sized rock in his slingshot a Tibetan can kill a wild dog, a wolf, or even a bandit from a distance of fifty yards!

Tibetan men and women dress alike, in a warm gown called a *chu-ba*, which reaches to the knees. It can be made of a matted wool which is almost waterproof, or of animal skin. But the gowns seldom have pockets. All articles are stuffed inside the upper portion of the gown, where a kind of pouch is sewn in to store things.

If the life of a herdsman is harsh, the life of a Tibetan farmer is equally so. The altitude of his land determines which crops can be planted. Tibet is the highest of all countries, with an average elevation of some 16,000 feet, and it is often called "the roof of the world." The only grain that can grow at an altitude of 14,000 feet is barley, and for that reason it has become the staple crop of the Tibetans. At lower altitudes wheat and buckwheat can grow, and, still lower, hardy corn is planted. Most other vegetables and fruits are almost unknown.

The altitude also determines the length of the growing season. In the higher regions the time of warm weather is relatively short. Above 14,000 feet the barley does not have a chance to ripen before the cold comes, so it is not good quality. Still, the farmers plant it so that the crop can be used as fodder for the animals. The diet of farmers in the Mekong area is not much different from that of the nomadic herdsmen.

A herdsman with his sling. *(Office of Tibet)*

Another reason for poor farming conditions is the lack of rainfall. The monsoon winds of India and lower China cannot rise above the towering Himalayas. Tibet is mostly an arid country, with an average yearly precipitation of about eight inches. Farmers use irrigation methods, but the small mountain streams they tap do not have much water, and in winter they are frozen.

In the region of the three rivers it is not hard for a Tibetan to acquire land for a farm. For this is the "country of the twenty-five tribes," whose people are subjects of the king of the Nang-Chen. The Nang-Chen king is also the chief of the largest tribe. He has very little power over the others. At times the tribes fight against each other and the king can do nothing to stop the battles. Nobody really knows how many people are in all the tribes, but in 1930, when the last count was made, there were about 75,000.

The land in each particular area belongs either to the chief of a tribe or to the lamasery. Any tribesman can apply to the chief for some land and get it, if he agrees to cultivate it. The land itself is free, but after three years taxes must be paid. Under the ancient laws three-fifths of the crop goes to the chief. Also, the farmer must work on the chief's land before he works on his own, and he is paid in barley flour for his labor. The farmer, in turn, can lease out his own land to someone else, or have someone sharecrop.

In many parts of Tibet, including the Mekong region, polyandry is practiced. This means that a woman can have more than one husband. Men outnumber women in those sections of the country, so polyandry is a matter of practicality for them.

The young boys and girls along the Mekong do not go to school. Whatever education they do get comes during the time they serve in a lamasery. They might possibly learn to write, using an alphabet which is similar to the Sanskrit of India. They also learn some reading, in order to read the daily prayers. But that is all. Formal education among the people of the Mekong headwaters is all but unknown.

Traveling through the Kham region we may see numerous tiny flecks of gold washing through the small streams. The Kham region —and probably many other parts of Tibet as well—contains a great many precious minerals. The Tibetans know the minerals are there, and sometimes a few of them might pan for gold to use in decorations and ornaments. Otherwise, gold has no meaning for them. They don't buy anything and all their wealth is counted in animal herds or food-producing land. Copper or any other metal that can be made into utensils is valued. Little mining is done in remote Tibet. It would be too difficult to bring the needed heavy machinery over the high mountain ranges.

The people of the Upper Mekong often suffer from stomach pains due to the lack of a balanced diet. Many have goiter, which is a swelling of the neck glands. Fish or iodized salt would help cure that disease, but there isn't much fish in the streams of the mountains and plateaus, and Tibetans are lucky to get any salt at all. Being a superstitious people they try to cure themselves with their charms and amulets, or with certain herbs which they believe have magical healing powers. There are no doctors, hospitals, or clinics, or any other practice of modern medicine in that desolate upland country.

A favorite Tibetan medicine is a kind of black fungus plant the Chinese call *chung ts'ao*, meaning "insect plant." It comes from a species of caterpillar which spins a tight cocoon around itself and never emerges. Because of the way the cocoon is attached to the plant it seems to be sprouting right out of the plant itself. Small boys go hunting for *chung ts'ao,* which fetches a good price.

Almost from the point where the Mekong left its source, it has been descending gradually. It started at a height of 16,400 feet; at Chamdo it is about 10,000 feet. The deep trenches through which the Mekong flows look the same, the water seems unchanged from its brackish-brown color of before. Now, however, travel is easier, for it is not as hard to breathe, and the mountains, while still high, do not tower up as forbiddingly.

Just below Chamdo are many mud watchtowers, built more than five hundred years ago by a Likiang-Nashi tribal chief, used to warn one village against surprise attacks by another. From the tops of the towers some of these villages can be seen in the distance. They bear a strange resemblance to the Hopi Indian villages of the American Southwest, with their flat roofs and the corn spread on the roofs to dry in the sun. Along the roads leading in and out of the villages are numerous statues and small stone pyramids, carved with figures and the words of prayers.

Soon the Mekong flows out of Tibet into China. It is impossible to say exactly where this happens, for there is no boundary line. It is still the same wild, barren, yet somehow beautiful country of the Himalaya mountains.

CHAPTER 3

The Mekong in China and Burma

There is no real boundary between Tibet and China. However, if there were a boundary, it would be a small stream which comes down from the heights of sacred Dokerla Pass. The pass itself is a narrow precipitous trail that leads over mountains toward the Salween River. In times past many Buddhist pilgrims committed suicide by throwing themselves off Dokerla Pass, for to die on that holy spot meant emancipation and deliverance from being born again. Some religious monks did nothing all year but cross and recross Dokerla, and they did it by the measurement of their bodies. They lay flat on the ground, arms outstretched over their heads. Then they rose, placed their feet at the point reached by their outstretched fingers and lay flat again. Such a crossing took months to complete, but the monks considered it a sacred duty.

Another way to tell the difference between Tibet and China is in the name given the Mekong River. The Tibetans call it Dzachu or Nam Chu. The Chinese call it Lants'ang Kiang—"the turbulent river." The river itself was unknown to the ancient Chinese. It was not until the eighteenth century that the Chinese began to explore it.

The Chinese provinces of Sikang and Yünnan, through which the Mekong flows, are part of the great Tibetan-Shan plateau. The entire region is a mixture of high mountains, deep valleys, long and level plateaus, and it contains some of the most beautiful scenery to be found in Asia. Yünnan has been called by some explorers "the Switzerland of China" because of its rolling hills, its mountains swinging away from level tableland, its swift-flowing streams. This is still high country, with altitudes averaging from 5,000 to 8,000 feet above sea level.

These Chinese provinces also have a climate much different from that of Tibet. The headwater country of the Kham region is bitter cold in winter, but northern Yünnan has a much more even and temperate climate. Many travelers maintain that this region has the best all-around climate in China. Summer temperatures climb to about 85 degrees and winters are moderate. There is not much rainfall in Sikang and upper Yünnan, which keeps the humidity low—except in the Mekong gorges, where the same malarial conditions still prevail.

Any attempt to describe the people of Sikang and Yünnan is extremely difficult because of the many different hill tribes scattered throughout the provinces. For example, in Yünnan there are nearly eighteen million people, of which more than six million are not Chinese. These six million can be broken down into more than

Pumi tribesmen in Yünnan.

fifty different minority tribes, most of whom live in western Yünnan and comprise the majority of people living near the Mekong.

Part of this great mixture of peoples is due to the conquests of the Mongol war lord Kublai Khan in the thirteenth century. His huge armies were sent out to conquer China, and in large measure they succeeded. As a result, a number of changes took place, which altered the population of southwestern China. First, the people who lived there, the Thais, fled from Yünnan into parts of Burma and present-day Thailand. Second, other emperors, seeking to stop the invaders, imported mercenary soldiers from western India. They remained in the area after the battles were over and married Yünnan women. The Indian soldiers brought with them the Moslem religion. Today, their descendants are Chinese in every respect but religion; they have remained Moslem. Third, a good number of the

Lutzu tribesman, from Yünnan, experiments in college chemistry laboratory.

Mongols of Kublai Khan's army also stayed in Yünnan and they, too, married women of the region.

Many centuries ago some southern Tibetans moved into Sikang and northern Yünnan and intermarried with the mountain people of the P'u tribes. This mixture, along with some others, produced a tribe called Wumans, who are dark skinned.

But these are only a small part of the incredibly complex tribes of the Sikang and Yünnan provinces. Some of them are extremely primitive to this day. Dr. Frank Kingdon Ward, the British botanist, one of the earliest explorers of the Mekong in China and Tibet, tells of hearing about a tribe who lived in trees with monkeys, for their country (in southern Yünnan, between the Salween and Irrawaddy rivers, west of the Mekong) was a swamp full of snakes and tigers. They wore no clothes because they did not know how to sew. Other tribes traded with them twice a year, although what these primitive people had to trade was never mentioned.

Of all the tribes we would encounter on our journey down the Mekong valley of western China, the Lolos are most numerous. They are probably the most civilized as well. Lolos have a written language of some three thousand words, which are used mostly for religious purposes. Actually, Lolo is a common word in southwestern China and it means "small basket." Perhaps they got their name from a certain superstitious custom: On their tombs they erect a pole and place a basket on top of it; the basket is the dwelling place for the spirit of the dead person. Both men and women of the tribe dress the same, in gray felt cloaks fastened around the neck and falling below the knees.

While the various groups of Lolos may have many similar cus-

Lolo girl with corn.

Lolo girl makes a woodcut.

toms, not all of them are alike. Their appearance and occupations can also be quite different. In some regions, the so-called "Black Lolos" sell only fuel, while in others the "White Lolos" raise and sell corn, and it has been that way for many years.

To add to the confusion caused by the bewildering profusion of varied peoples in southwestern China is the fact that parts of tribes are so widely scattered. For example, there are Lolos in southern Tibet, there are Lolos in northern Burma a thousand miles to the south, and Lolos in between. And the same can be said for many of the other tribes.

What sort of people are these tribesmen? How do they differ from each other? To name only a few of the tribes and their characteristics might show why Yünnan province is spoken of as "China's Wild West":

Chinese social worker cuts Yao children's hair.

There are the primitive Lisu who hunt with crossbows and use their hair as a quiver for arrows.

There are the Yao who live in the hills and used to be cave dwellers.

There are the Nashi, whose men wear green stone ornaments as earrings.

And, around the region of southern Yünnan, there are the peaceful Shans, the stolid Chins, the fierce, warlike Kachins, the "tame" Wa, and the "wild" Wa and the Nagas, both of whom are head-hunters.

The savage Wa tribesmen chop off heads for two reasons: as a sacrifice to the god of agriculture in order to assure a good harvest, and to appease the evil spirits and ward off plagues. One of their special targets is the Han-Chinese people, who consider themselves superior to any of the minority tribes. European explorers who came to Wa territory learned very soon that this area was not safe. To this day no one governs or controls these people, or even tries to.

The multiplicity of tribes in China's Wild West is confusing. But, in a way, it is no more confusing than America's Wild West might have been to a European who visited the United States a hundred years ago. He, too, might have been puzzled at hearing about the variety of American Indians: the Cherokee, Chickasaw, and Seminole of the Southeast, the Osage, Pawnee and Omaha of the Plains, the Apaches, Hopis and Navahos of the southwest, and all the other Indian tribes that once inhabited America.

The Was cut off heads, American Indians took scalps. The primitive Lisu hunt with crossbows, United States Indians used ordi-

Girls from the Wa tribe.

Kachin and Thais repair irrigation ditch for their rice paddies.

nary bows. The Yao are extremely backward, the Indians of the New World had never seen a wheel until Europeans brought it to America's shores. The simple Miaos of Yünnan live in fear of demons, all Indians believed in evil spirits.

For the most part the Mekong people of Sikang and Yünnan follow the same occupations as the inhabitants of Tibet's Kham region: farming and raising animals. However, both the herds and crops are different. Most of the Chinese herds consist of sheep and goats, with few yaks. The farmers raise a good deal of corn, plus wheat, tea, tobacco, fruits, nuts, and, in the areas of lower Yünnan where the monsoon winds reach, rice. In most cases the farmers' houses are built into the mountain sides, and in order to tend their crops they have to descend to their farms, which are on a lower level.

There is little mechanized industry in Yünnan, but there is a good deal of mining. Once, the province was noted for its rich copper mines, and, even today, copper, tin, coal, and other minerals are taken from the mountains in large quantities. There are also some precious stones to be mined—jade, turquoise, and rubies.

If there is one quality these mountain tribesmen possess in large measure it is courage. This was proved beyond any doubt during World War II with the building of the Burma Road spur—the Ledo Road, later called the Stilwell Road.

Since ancient times it had been all but impossible to go overland from China to Burma due to the mountain ranges, the deep river gorges, and the sickness that lurked in the valleys of the Mekong and Salween rivers. Even the great conqueror Kublai Khan was unable to overrun Burma for that reason. He sent an army of half

48

a million troops to invade Burma, but half his men never got across the mountains. They died of disease and in battle against the hill tribesmen, and finally the remnants of his forces had to turn back.

In the twentieth century a road was begun, connecting Lashio in Burma with Kunming, capital of Yünnan province. It took years to build, but the road was opened in 1938.

When World War II started, invading Japanese forces drove up into lower Burma and captured part of the road, up to the China border. The Allies had to construct a new approach in order to supply China with goods and war materials. Meanwhile, cargo planes were flying "over the hump" of the lower Himalayas, crossing jungles and the Salween and Mekong rivers.

Late in 1942, construction was begun on the new spur road. To bring in heavy road-building equipment was impossible For more than two years more than a million hill tribesmen of Burma and China, working under U.S. army engineers, hacked out the road across the mountains, gorges, and jungles, using rakes, shovels, baskets—and their bare hands. They knew full well that crossing the river ravines meant exposing themselves to the dreaded fevers, but they took the risk and paid dearly. It was later estimated that out of every 250 workers, 200 fell ill with malaria and most of them soon died. But nothing could stop the construction. Finally, in 1945, after the Japanese had been driven from middle Burma, the road opened for traffic. It led from Ledo in eastern India, across Burma, through the low foothills and mountain passes, across the Salween and Mekong and into the heart of Yünnan. Strong suspension bridges had been thrown across both rivers. Later, high officials of the Allied armies surveyed the road and declared, "Only the brave Chinese could have accomplished that feat in such a short time!"

For hundreds of miles the Salween, Mekong, and Yangtze have followed parallel courses, from Tibet, through Sikang and northern Yünnan. As the trio of rivers reaches central Yünnan and the outskirts of the region where monsoon winds blow, the Yangtze begins a long, looping turn to the east and northeast, to follow a new course into the very heart of China. It finally ends its 3,200-mile journey in the East China Sea, just above the great city of Shanghai.

The Salween and Mekong continue their side-by-side courses for perhaps another hundred miles or more. Just north of the town of Paoshan they begin to slip away from each other. It was there, according to an account written by Marco Polo, the Venetian traveler, that twelve thousand soldiers of Kublai Khan defeated sixty thousand Burmese and their war elephants. This disaster brought ruin to the ancient Burmese city of Pagan, which was a magnificent place with some five thousand shrines. The Mongol legions, however, could not move farther across the mountains and jungles of the Burma border.

The gap between the Salween and Mekong widens considerably as the rivers course on, and then the Salween enters Burma in the northeastern section of the country, runs along the eastern mountain region bordering Thailand, and empties into the Gulf of Martaban.

The Mekong continues its unnavigable course through the rest of Yünnan, almost to its southernmost tip, and at last reaches the jutting spur of land where Laos and Burma come together. For some 130 miles more the Mekong flows between these two countries, its waters being the border between them. Stretching away from the rocky ravines on both sides of the banks is dense jungle, alive with the rustle and sounds of savage animals. There are still no people in the vicinity of the river, not even the wild Wa.

Then the Mekong swerves abruptly to the east, to begin its run through the nations that depend on the river for their livelihood. Half of its journey is done.

CHAPTER 4

The Mekong in Laos and Thailand

The kingdom of Laos has about 2,300,000 people. Approximately one quarter of them live in the mountain regions. All the rest make their home along the Mekong River and its branches.

The ruler of Laos is King Savang Vanthana, who is also the head of the army and supreme Buddhist religious authority. He appoints the prime minister. There is a National Assembly which is elected by the people for a five-year term.

Laos, too, has its legend that tells how the people came to that land. Many centuries ago, their story goes, a semi-god named Khun Borom came down from the sky on a white elephant, with all his wealth and his two wives. When he reached a spot near what is now the city of Dien Bien Phu in North Vietnam, he saw a strange vine bearing two huge gourds. He pierced the gourds and out sprang men, women, animals, seeds, and all sorts of useful things. Full of curiosity and wishing to hasten the miracle, he burned a hole in the gourds with a hot poker. Out leaped the Kha tribesmen, their skins darker because they were covered with soot, which, the legend says, remains on their skins to this very day.

Khun Borom had seven sons, and when he died his vast empire was divided among them. The eldest son, Khun Lo, inherited the kingdom of Lan-Xang, which means "land of a million elephants." Later the kingdom was broken up and much of it was incorporated into what is now Thailand. The part of Khun Lo's kingdom remaining formed Laos as it is today.

Many legends have *some* truth in them, as does this one. The tale of the gourds, of course, is simply a folk story. However, scholars have learned that Khun Borom did exist and there really was a kingdom of Lan-Xang. In those days, many centuries in the past, China was often referred to as "the Celestial Empire," and no doubt that was why the legend relates that Khun Borom came from the sky. But there were people in Laos long before he arrived. In fact the whole history of Asia is filled with migrating peoples, wars, mixtures of races, and changing boundaries.

As far back as the sixth century B.C. the Chinese talked about "the barbarians beyond the Yangtze." These were the Khas, a warlike, savage people. The Khas were defeated by the kingdom of Champa, a nation in the middle of Indochina, and they scattered into the hills, where they live today. Champa, in turn, was conquered by the Khmers, the people of Cambodia, who absorbed the Chams into their own culture. Next the Thais came (perhaps this was the time of Khun Borom) and they wrested control of the territory. The kingdom of Lan-Xang, given to Khun Lo, contained what is now Laos, Thailand, Cambodia, and all of North and South Vietnam, making it a truly powerful kingdom. Later a second wave of Thais came from lower Yünnan, fleeing the legions of Kublai Khan. Many of this second group of Thais went around Laos and settled in Siam (now called Thailand). Thus the peoples of Laos and Thailand have common ancestors from south China. They both are Buddhist and have similar languages.

Many bloody wars splintered Lan-Xang. At various times parts of the region were under the control of Burma, Thailand and Annam (today comprising North and South Vietnam). Late in the nineteenth century the French came to Indochina, and it was not until 1954 that they were finally forced to leave, after their defeat at Dien Bien Phu. Their influence is still felt today. French is an accepted language in Laos, Cambodia, and Vietnam, especially among the better-educated people of these countries.

After serving as a border river separating Laos from Burma, the Mekong continues to perform the same function as a boundary between Laos and Thailand. No people live on its banks here, either, for it is still a wild torrent, about three hundred yards wide, running through heavily forested mountain ravines. The only living things present to appreciate its natural beauty are a wide variety of animals: tigers and elephants, leopards and cobras, lizards and alligators.

The Mekong means much more to Laos than it does to Thailand. In Laos it is "the Royal Road," for there are few dependable land roads (and no railroads) in that underdeveloped country. The river furnishes the best available means of transportation, even though

54

The Mekong near Luang Prabang, Laos. *(United Nations)*

it is not navigable in a number of places, especially in the upper regions near Burma and northern Laos. Since most of its people live along the banks, it is the handiest "road" for everybody.

In Thailand, the Mekong, while of some significance, is still only a border river. The Chao Phraya is Thailand's chief river.

It is only when the Mekong leaves the Thai border and curves into the interior of Laos that, at long last, there are signs of human beings on its shores. There are still mountains surrounding the river, but now they are pushed back from the water's edge. Tiny hamlets appear; first a few houses grouped together, and then larger villages, until finally the Mekong flows past the first city built along its shores, the royal Laotian capital, Luang Prabang.

Laos has two capitals: the royal capital, where the king's palace is situated, and the administrative capital, Vientiane, where most of the day-to-day government work is done.

By ordinary standards Luang Prabang is not a large city. It has a population estimated between 15,000 and 20,000, but it is a thriving metropolis, mixing ancient and modern ways of life. There is a good-sized airport to add to the city's activity as a trade center. Luang Prabang carries on a thriving commerce in rice, silk, rubber, timber, gum, and resins. Many ancient pagodas and Buddhist temples overlook the now slower-moving Mekong. Along the shores and in midstream are sampans and pirogues, the latter being a kind of boat made from a single hollowed-out log.

The Buddhist temples play an important role in the lives of all the Indochinese, especially in Laos. Perhaps that is why Laotians often say, "Laos, like Ceylon, is a land of monks." They believe that every Buddhist male should spend at least a little time in a pagoda as a novice, and most of the men do so.

Village house outside Luang Prabang. *(United Nations)*

A chief priest of Laos.

Before Buddhism came to Laos, the people practiced a form of spirit worship called "the cult of Phi." *Phi* ("spirit") still holds a strong place in their beliefs. According to this belief everything contains a spirit—streams, rocks, chairs—even ideas and thoughts. The forests, they believe, are full of evil tree spirits, and it can be dangerous to remain among the trees at night, all alone.

Buddhism came to Laos during the reign of Fa Ngum, and his story is one of the heroic sagas of Laotian tradition because it is true. Some time about the year 1320, Fa Ngum's father was driven out of his kingdom by his own father, because of what was described as "loose living." Fa Ngum and his father sought refuge in Cambodia. When Fa Ngum was sixteen, he married a Khmer princess. Later, he and his father returned as conquerors to the kingdom they had left. By that time Fa Ngum had been converted to Buddhism by his wife, and they took with them many religious objects, including a gold Buddha statue over 500 years old, which was called Phra Bang ("Protector of the Kingdom"). Phra Bang became the revered symbol of Buddhism in Laos, and it still is.

Despite all their devotion to Buddhism, many Laotians still believe in the witch doctors of their ancestors. They have a great fear of evil sorcerers; such wicked magicians, they believe, can cause an object to enter a victim's body, even if the sorcerers themselves are far away. The object can be an old chicken bone, a pebble, a slice of buffalo hide, and unless the foreign object is removed the suffering person might die. Then a good witch doctor is summoned, for he has the power to overcome the sorcerer. The witch doctor holds a lighted candle in one hand and a betel leaf in the other, which he passes over the victim's body, muttering "magic"

59

An ancient, abandoned Buddhist temple in the Plain of Jars, Laos.

words, until he locates the foreign object. Then he lays the betel leaf on the spot, says a few more magic words to bring it under the surface of the skin, and tries to bite it out of the victim's body.

Any traveler journeying down the lower Mekong in Laos is almost sure to find himself in the midst of some kind of festival. Almost anything can be an excuse for a celebration: a religious holiday, a wedding, a birth, the start of harvest, the end of harvest, the opening of the fishing season—or even a funeral. Laotians look upon death as a good thing, for the soul will enter Nirvana and a new and better life.

For many years Laotians did not have last names. Children were given only one name, such as "Gold," "Palm Tree," or "Blossom." If two people had the same name, the father would add his son's or daughter's name to his, so that a man might be called "Mr. Palm Tree, father of Blossom." If the man had no children he added his wife's name, making his name "Mr. Palm Tree, husband of River." In the case of a bachelor, who had no wife or children, there was often confusion. In 1943, by a government decree, the people of Laos adopted last names.

The Laotians are farmers and rice is their chief crop. Rice is the great staple food of nearly all of Asia, and the Mekong provides enough wet fields for the paddies. Other crops include tobacco, sugar cane, corn, and a variety of vegetables.

The Laotians have learned to live with the monsoon season, which lasts from the sporadic April thundershowers, through the torrential downpours of July and August, when it seems that there will never be an end to the deluge, and on through mid-November when the rains abate. Flooded villages are common during the monsoons. But the people know that soon the waters will recede, and afterward the Mekong region will see little rainfall until the next year's monsoons. Meanwhile, as the rivers are full, that is the time to start fishing in earnest.

All during its run through Tibet and China, there has been little fishing in the Mekong waters. Even if fishermen could survive the malaria in the ravines, the dashing currents, hurtling over rocks, would rip the nets to shreds. This is not the case in the lower Mekong. The people along the banks can feast on the many varieties of fish to be found in the river. One of the most prized catches is the *pa boeuk*, a kind of sheatfish (really a form of catfish) which sometimes grows to a length of six and a half feet.

In Laotian legend is a story, not only about the *pa boeuk*, but also about how the Mekong was formed. Once there were two dragon spirits who lived near each other and were good neighbors. One day one of them killed an elephant and had his servants bring half of it to his friend. Some time later, the second dragon spirit killed a porcupine, and thought to return the favor by sending half of it to the first spirit. When the first dragon spirit saw that he was being repaid for his great gift with half of a very small animal, he became angry. However, it was unthinkable that they should fight. Instead, he sent a challenge to his neighbor: "Let us see which of us can dig through the land and be first to reach the sea!" The challenge was accepted. The spirit who hollowed out the bed of the Mekong won, and he brought back with him the *pa boeuk*. The other spirit hollowed out the Menam or Chao Phraya in Thailand, where there are no catfish.

Laotians seldom fish alone. Usually, whole families join forces, and sometimes one village or even several villages get together for a huge fishing festival. Strangely enough, the people will seldom try to catch more fish than a family can eat in a day or two. As a result there is not much fish for sale in village markets. If a family does have some fish left over, it is carefully preserved, whole, in a mixture of salt and ricebran. The Laotians call this briny fish *padek,* and it tides them over when they have no fresh fish. When the Mekong's waters are low and the fish supply dwindles, the people try their luck in nearby streams and ponds.

Forestry is a potential industry for Mekong dwellers, for Laos has many huge stands of trees, including the prized teak, so valuable for making fine furniture. However, Laotians themselves have not yet benefited from this natural resource. The French devastated the forests, chopping down great numbers of teak trees. The logs were floated down the Mekong, over the rapids and falls, until they were picked up at Phnom Penh in Cambodia, or Saigon in Vietnam. There was no other way for the French to get the logs to market, for Laos is a landlocked country. It is surrounded on all sides by other countries: Burma, China, North Vietnam, South Vietnam, Cambodia, and Thailand. Today, those teak logs felled by Laotians are exported to Thailand and from there to other parts of the world.

Otherwise, the people of Laos use the surrounding forests for their own daily needs. Bamboo is used to build their houses, wood oil for lighting, some woodland plants and roots for food. Branches are turned into household equipment, such as brooms. Wood is used for heat and cooking. Gums and resins are needed to build boats and make roofs waterproof.

Except for some small rice mills and brickworks, there is no real industry in Laos. In all the more than 9,000 villages in the country, people make things for themselves. Every house has a loom to spin cloth for the family's clothing, and some of the articles are very artistic. Many Laotian women are expert at making silk scarves embroidered with gold and silver threads; long, flowing multicolored skirts; exquisite ceremonial sarongs. In fact these pieces of clothing are so beautiful and well made that there is a growing demand for them in the Western world, and the manufacture of some of these decorative articles is rapidly becoming a cottage industry.

What is life in the villages of Laos really like? Only a native of the land could really explain it and make the people, the animals, and the land itself come to life; as in this poem by Khamchan Pradith, the United Nations Counsellor of Laos:

LIFE IN A LAO VILLAGE

Creeping through narrow valleys like a big snake,
Rolling its mud and gravel against rocks,
Along its grassy banks browse deer flocks,
The Mekong River flows into the Khmer Lake.
On steep mountains with high peaks,
Among bushy trees towering the blue sky
Thousands of birds which sing, chirp and fly
Beating their wings on the top of teaks.

When the sun piercing early dew flashes its rays,
When the villagers harness their buffaloes,

When morn fire escaping thatched huts glows
The whole pagoda wakes up and prays.
Some fishermen shivering in their boats row,
From time to time thunder their doleful cry;
Naive girls sing, laugh, husk their paddy nearby
Teasing each other, they talk about their "beau."

Under the shady banyan, a husky man nets;
Near him, his wife spins and talks;
Toward a coconut tree, another woman walks
To help her son weave bamboo baskets.

I observe a blackbird pulling thatch twigs,
Fluttering here and there, then disappears quietly.
A peacock spreads out its tail proudly
So suddenly that it frightens two pigs.
From the ricefield edge, on a bumpy path
Comes an oxcart full of yellow hay,
Blowing a purple dust many yards away
While three elephants take their bath.

The sun, at its zenith is dreadfully burning;
The whole village noiselessly seeks shelter,
Except a few children patting the limpid water
Jauntily one after another they are running.
Little by little the day hearth lowers
And the thick jungle seems to be afire,
The heavens change into a big sapphire,
Back to the Mekong banks come the rowers.

The monsoon wind furiously swings palm trees
Blowing the water surface in big waves,
Bats hurriedly flapping out their caves
Darken the sky like the swarm of bees.

Doves, herons, storks, robins, sparrows
At full speed fly down the river streams
In the depth of my heart reach their screams
As if never again would come hopeful tomorrow.

Goodbye to the twilight, the bonzes recite their prayer
Mingling their psalms to the spinning wheels;
A tiger bellowing rises from some remote hills;
That's Lao village life on the Mekong River.

For 373 miles, as the Mekong River continues its twisting, curving course in Laos, other streams continue to join it, waterways from the upland plateaus where other tribes live. One such tribe is the Meo. The women twist their hair into high knots. They wear black blouses, pleated, striped skirts and leggings that wrap around their ankles and shins. These women know the value of precious metals. They wear large silver earrings and huge numbers of silver necklaces. Sometimes a woman may have as much as ten pounds of silver around her neck and in her ears. This is their security, a kind of "bank account" that they can carry with them wherever they go.

When the Mekong reaches the town of Pak Lay, it moves due south toward Thailand again. Once it reaches the border, the river begins a meandering course once more, serving anew as the Thai-

A Meo tribal village.

Thai girl tending one of many vegetable gardens along the Mekong.
(United Nations)

Woman spinning in Chonabot, a village in northeast Thailand.
(*United Nations*)

Laotian boundary. It is in this section of the Mekong, with the Thais and Laotians living side by side, that the great similarity between them can be seen. Perhaps the interior tribes differ, but the Mekong Thais and Laotians are very much alike, in religion, customs, language, and appearance.

The Thais, too, have strong beliefs in evil spirts that carry sickness. They share with the Laotians a theory about medicine that is strange to Western ideas. According to their belief, the human body is composed of four elements: wind, water, fire, and earth. It is the lack of balance in the body of these elements that causes all sorts of sickness. For example, too much "earth" in the joints is the real cause of rheumatism. Charms, amulets, talismans, and sometimes tattoos are all useful in warding off evil spirits.

There are a number of towns spotted along the Mekong's banks in this region. The river is wide and mostly navigable. When the water is low some sandbars lie exposed, and gold dust has been panned from these spits of dry ground. In some sections of the river, deep digging into these sandbars has produced sapphires and other gems. But it takes courage to go hunting for minerals, for the stretches between towns are infested with tigers, leopards, and elephants, all of whom come down to the banks of the river to drink.

The first really modern city along the Mekong's banks is Vientiane, the administrative capital of Laos, with its bustling population of about 100,000. Here there is no jungle covering the banks of the Mekong. Rather the land is like strips of plains, land which is fertile and flooded by shallow rice paddies.

In the seventeenth century, the empire of Lan-Xang was split into

The Mekong near Vientiane, Laos. (*United Nations*)

two kingdoms. Vientiane became a kingdom by itself, with its capital being the city of the same name. In 1827, when the Thais seized control, the city of Vientiane was almost destroyed, and only a few old pagodas were left standing. It was rebuilt and once more became an important river port and trade center, doing a brisk business in teak and other hardwoods, in textiles, the skins of leopards and other animals, in benzoin, which is used as a perfume base, and stick-lac, a gum produced by tree parasites and necessary in the making of certain kinds of varnish.

Travel between Luang Prabang, the royal capital, and Vientiane, the administrative capital, is not always possible via the Mekong route. In monsoon season, the swollen river sweeps along too fast for even the power boats that are sometimes used around Vientiane. In the dry season, there is danger of getting hung up on

Vientiane flooded by the Mekong.

Khone Falls, in Laos, near the Cambodian border. *(United Nations)*

a sandbar, or from the rapids which are scattered along the river bed. Also, below Vientiane, a number of rivers from Thailand pour into the Mekong. Thus, the Mekong becomes a raging torrent again as it moves steadily south, traveling as before through trenches and gorges. One particularly difficult section is the Khone Falls. Here the Mekong forms a roaring cascade that is eight miles wide!

After a long course following the contours of the Thai-Laos border, the Mekong drops away from Thailand and runs a more peaceful course toward Cambodia. It is almost as if the mighty Mekong were anxious to rush into another country, to see more of Indochina. And soon it does. In the vicinity of the town of Khong, the river leaves Laos and enters the land of the ancient Khmers, Cambodia.

CHAPTER 5

The Mekong in Cambodia

Like the rest of Indochina, Cambodia today is the result of ancient migrations, wars, the coming of missionaries from other countries, and mixtures of peoples.

At about the time of Jesus Christ there were three independent peoples living in the lower Mekong region: the Funanese, the Chams, and the Khmers. The first great cultural change came about when the educated Hindus came to Indochina from eastern India, and introduced their religion and alphabet.

For centuries, there were intermittent wars, during which control of the central part of Indochina changed hands. First the Funanese dominated, then the Chams, and finally, early in the ninth century, the Khmers emerged as supreme rulers. Their empire extended far into upper Indochina, and included much of what is today South Vietnam, Cambodia, a part of Thailand, and Laos.

The Khmers were great warriors. Sometimes they were referred to as "the Romans of the Orient," for, like the legions of Caesar conquering Europe, the Khmer armies brushed aside all opposition. And, like the Romans, the Khmers built some of the most beautiful and enduring cities and temples to be found anywhere in the world.

They established their capital at Angkor Thom, in central Cambodia, and erected a series of incredibly beautiful temples and other buildings, all intricately ornamented. In the center of the city stood Bayon, their national temple, with a great central tower, encircling galleries, and four huge portals, each one carved with a different face of Siva, one of the supreme Hindu gods. The whole building was surrounded by a moat and a wall. Yet, even this magnificent temple and the surrounding palaces were second in beauty to another temple, Angkor Wat, located about a mile south of the city. Built more than nine hundred years ago of various colored sandstone and limonite blocks, Angkor Wat is acknowledged as the outstanding achievement in all of the Khmers' architecture.

Among the peoples conquered by the Khmers were the Thais. In the thirteenth century the Thais rose up against their overlords and began a series of revolutions that finally brought the power of the Khmers to an end.

The first Europeans to come to Cambodia were the Portuguese traders, who arrived in the sixteenth century. Then came the Dutch, and finally, in the middle of the nineteenth century, the French established themselves. They remained until after World War II, when Cambodia became an independent nation.

The kingdom of Cambodia today is about the size of the state of Washington. The chief executive of the country is Prince Noro-dom Sihanouk, whose powers are exercised through his council of ministers. There is a legislature which is elected by the people. Most of the Cambodians live either along the shores of the Mekong, or near the Tonle Sap Lake and Tonle Sap River.

The Mekong flows into Cambodia through forest land, and lumbering has become an important industry. In the northern part of the country, near the town of Kratie, lumberjacks can be seen heaving logs into the Mekong, from which point they float down-river to Phnom Penh. There, other lumberjacks will saw them into a size convenient for shipment or use. Many of the Phnom Penh lumberjacks live with their families in palm-leaf shelters built on large rafts made of bamboo or hardwood. These rafts ply between Kratie and Phnom Penh so that the workers can be at hand for their jobs.

Rubber is another important source of income for Cambodia. The huge rubber plantations were begun by the French, and for many years provided a good portion of the world's rubber supply.

Most Cambodians, however, are engaged in farming, and the country is rich in rice. A number of other crops are grown, including corn, beans, peanuts, sesame, manioc, bananas, citrus fruits, and mangoes. Additional cash crops are tobacco, cotton, kapok, and sugar palm.

The farm and peasant houses, especially those along the river banks, are built on stilts, sometimes ten feet high, since monsoon rains make the waters rise almost overnight. Some houses have partitions to form a number of rooms, but more often there is just one large room where everybody sleeps, cooks, eats, and does daily

Cambodian children weed a garden. *(United Nations)*

household chores. The carts, looms, and the various forms of live-stock (buffalo, pigs, chickens) are kept under the house. Usually, the clump of thatch-roofed houses that make up a village are clustered around a pagoda.

Most Cambodian farms are small, and therefore many farmers cannot afford to buy a tractor. But they manage to get around that by renting one when it is needed. Enterprising businessmen buy tractors and make a handsome profit leasing them out to various farmers for a few days at a time. Cambodian farmers are progressive in other ways, too. They raise enough rice for export, but have come to realize that European markets prefer certain varieties of rice which the Cambodians themselves do not particularly care for. With government help, they have begun to experiment with different varieties of rice for shipment abroad.

The Cambodian farmers have little difficulty getting their crops to world markets, for here the Mekong is wide, navigable, truly an important lifeline of traffic and communications. In upper Laos, around Luang Prabang, only smaller craft can move about the Mekong regularly. In upper Cambodia, the Mekong's traffic is made up of a wide variety of boats: barges, junks, sampans, pirogues, and even some motorboats. At Phnom Penh, small steamers and freighters dock daily. However, Cambodians have learned that due to the changing river tides the Mekong is still full of tricks when it comes to loading or unloading cargo. Floating wharves are often used, jutting out from the banks to the side of the ship, so that, regardless of the tide, ship and wharf will remain at a fairly constant level.

It is not hard to know when our imaginary trip down the Me-

Typical sampan along the Mekong River at Phnom Penh, Cambodia.
(*United Nations*)

kong brings us to Phnom Penh. First the buildings come into view, then girls selling lotus seeds from gondolas are seen gliding along the waters. Oil tankers are pulling in and out of the floating wharves. The river is dotted with large junks and sampans, with families living on them. Finally the waterfront is directly ahead. Great stone steps, guarded by stone cobras with seven heads, lead up from the quays and into the streets of the city.

By far the most outstanding sight in Phnom Penh, one that can be seen from far off, is the famous "Wat Phnom," which means "Hill Temple." It is a striking structure, towering atop a hill, one of the most beautiful temples in all Indochina.

Cambodians say that about six hundred years ago, at the time when the Thais were beginning their revolutions against the Khmers, the rainy season flood waters washed a huge koki tree onto the hillside home of a lady named Penh. The tree was hollow, and inside the trunk she found four bronze Buddhas. The capital of Cambodia was at Angkor Thom, but people who heard of the incident and saw the four bronze Buddhas took it as a sign that the gods had abandoned Angkor Thom. Seeking a new capital, they chose the area where the four Buddhas had come to rest. In order to give the statues a place of honor, the lady Penh built a shrine atop her hill and a city sprang up around its base. It became the official capital later, when the invading Thais captured Angkor Thom, causing the king and his court to flee to the safety of the lady Penh's hill. Angkor Thom is a series of magnificent ruins now, a remembrance of the great civilization that flourished in the days of Khmer glory.

There is an air of bustling activity in the city of Phnom Penh.

A visitor wandering through the streets is likely to see barefoot Buddhist monks dressed in saffron-colored robes, holding yellow umbrellas as a shield from the sun. Old women, their heads shaved, honor their ancestors in ancient temples by burning whole clusters of incense sticks. They wear black *sampots*, which are ankle-length robes, and clean white blouses. Children are everywhere, flying kites, marching off to school, eating sunflower seeds or sugar-cane lollipops. Fishermen cast their nets off the waterfront quays into the murky waters of the brackish Mekong.

Nearly one third of Phnom Penh's residents are Chinese. They are Cambodia's tradesmen, shopkeepers, merchants. They play an extremely important role in the nation's commerce, buying, selling, trading, importing goods from countries all over the world. In a Chinese shop, for example, can be found Vietnamese cigarettes, Shanghai beer, some French or Viennese pastry, dogmeat sausage so dearly loved by the Indochinese. Other articles for sale include incense sticks, silver elephants, betel leaves, brass gongs, bamboo flutes, Chinese comic books, begging bowls, clothing from the West, clothing from the Orient, decorative dishes, and cooking pots.

Yet these international Chinese seldom, if ever, become citizens of Cambodia. They prefer to retain their own customs, language, and schools. These wishes are respected by the Cambodian government.

Among the busiest people in Phnom Penh are the fortunetellers who help people make important decisions. They spread out their oilcloth mats and exhibit their magic slates, copper amulets, a great variety of charms and mystical herbs. In their fortunetelling books are strange figures and symbols: a green-faced giant named Piphek; a half-man, half-bird named Garuda; the three-faced god, Chak Kboun, who sees past, present, and future. Elephants of various colors are in the book, and all have a different meaning. The fortunetellers consult the Cambodian calendar, which is based on the sun and the moon. The day of the week is taken into consideration, and each day has a different color. Cambodians take their fortunetelling seriously.

People in Phnom Penh love sports. Large crowds attend soccer and basketball games and flock to see prize fights. Boxing in Cambodia and Thailand is much different from that in the United States. There, it is perfectly legal to kick an opponent, and many prize fights have been won with a well-timed, smartly delivered kick in the face! Yet the contestants go into the ring wearing trunks and boxing gloves the same as Western boxers.

Travelers are often struck by the frequency with which the Cambodians smile. Perhaps it is because many people have gold teeth and wish to show them off. However, the real reason, undoubtedly, is their extreme politeness. When Cambodians meet they place their fingertips at about the level of their lips and make a half bow. It is their way of saying, "I greet and respect you, sir." The deeper the bow, the more respect and reverence is indicated for the person being greeted.

Although Cambodia was originally a Hindu country, the passage of time has changed that. Like all Indochinese countries, Cambodia is Buddhist. The people believe that every man over the age of sixteen must serve a term as a monk (called a bonze). The period of service can last for a few months, several years, or even a lifetime.

The religion and many of the superstitions are the same in all parts of Indochina. A common belief holds that spirits are everywhere. There is the firm conviction that man returns to life in another form after death, and it all depends on what sort of life that person has led before death. Everything is based on a system of merits and demerits. And one's deeds, good or bad, carry with them the seeds that will germinate in the new life. Thus, if something bad happens to a person, it may be due to the fact that he did something evil in a previous life and now it is catching up with him.

Cambodians are especially careful to guard against evil spirits harming their children. They frown upon anyone patting a child's head, for that is where the "soul stuff" is planted, and it can be harmed even by touching. The hair is also important, for it is a good hiding place for evil spirits. Many villagers shave their youngster's head, leaving only a center lock. When the child is older, at a time usually set by an astrologer, a monk shaves off this lock of hair too. That is the sign that the child is now an adult, and the hair is allowed to grow in again. If the child is sick, his name is changed so that the spirit of death will be confused and unable to find him. Cambodians, like Laotians, did not have last names for a long time. In 1910 a royal law decreed that all families must have last names, and they were to be used before the given name. Thus, by American standards, a man would be named Smith John or Jones William, instead of the other way around.

It is at Phnom Penh that the "Quatres Bras" ("Four Arms") is found. At this bend of the Mekong, two other rivers, the Bassac and Tonle Sap, meet to form a kind of large X. It is the combination of Tonle Sap (it means "Great Lake" in Cambodian) and the

Mekong which plays such an important role in the lives of Cambodia's people.

The Tonle Sap Lake lies in the west-central part of the country. From this large body of water flows the Tonle Sap River whose waters empty into the Mekong. During the monsoon season, when the rains pour additional water into the Mekong, the river rises high, in some years as much as forty-five feet. Then the full fury of the mighty Mekong is turned loose on the Cambodian countryside.

As the Mekong rushes along its swollen course, it literally stops the Tonle Sap River from flowing, backs it up and sends its water swiftly back to the lake from which it came. As the Tonle Sap comes gushing back, it overflows the Tonle Sap Lake, enlarging it tremendously, sometimes as much as fifteen times its previous size!

When the lake overflows, the forests, swamps, bogs, and streams in the vicinity are inundated. Many forest animals are caught in the floods, which cover great areas of formerly dry land. And the whole region actually becomes covered with enormous quantities of fish. They wash out into fields far from the lake, to remain there until the monsoon rains abate, the waters recede, and the people can come out after them in force. The rainy season turns the Tonle Sap region into one of Southeast Asia's great fishing regions. It has been estimated that the Tonle Sap, when flooded, yields ten times more fish per square mile of water than the fishing grounds of the North Atlantic!

The families of the Tonle Sap go wading or boating after the fish, armed with nets, baskets, and wicker scoops. They find fingerlings even in the tiniest puddles and dig down to pluck up wiggling

Village in Cambodia flooded by Mekong during monsoon.
(*Courtesy of the Shell Oil Co.*)

Fish traps on the Tonle Sap. (*United Nations*)

mudskippers, which survive low water by burrowing into the mud.

For the Cambodians, this is a "fish harvest," just as though they were bringing in rice, wheat, or some other crop. Fish are often harvested in "weirs," fences sometimes a mile long attached to boats, which prevent the fish from escaping. The fishermen throw their catch into hatches or baskets or whatever equipment they are working with.

Sometimes the lake is dotted with huge rafts, each of which contains a house and garden. The rafts are perhaps twenty feet long and made of bamboo, buoyed by large empty oil drums. The people raise herbs and vegetables in pots while the raft decks are covered with drying fish. Such rafts are really fish farms, which the natives call *trung trei*. Underneath the raft in a big "live box" are small fish that are fed corn mush so that they will grow big. It is estimated that perhaps 40,000 families live on raft houses or on stilt houses and engage in fishing. This is the time when they feast on one of the favorite dishes of the Indochinese, *nuoc nam sauce,* which is made with fermented juices of fish.

Watching over this scene of feverish activity from the middle of the lake is a temple of Takang, patron saint of the fishermen.

Fishing increases tremendously in the Mekong, too. Cambodians find sheatfish, the same as the Laotians do, except that in Cambodia it is called *trey reach.*

When the waters have passed the flood crest and receded, they leave behind in the Tonle Sap area a rich silt, excellent for growing all sorts of crops, so the farmers have vegetables and rice to go with the carp, chubs, eels, and other fish provided by overflow waters.

All through its run from Tibet, various large and small rivers have added their waters to the Mekong. The Tonle Sap is, in a way, the climax of all the tributaries that have flowed into the Mekong. Now, as if the river has more water than it needs, it begins to throw off tributaries of its own, forming several rivers and streams that branch away from the parent route. As the Mekong leaves Phnom Penh, it starts to form the great delta region the world has come to know as the "rice bowl of Asia." And it starts on the last leg of its long journey toward the South China Sea.

CHAPTER 6

The Mekong in South Vietnam

Ancient histories, which are part legend and part fact, say that in the year 2879 B.C. there was a kingdom called Van Lang. This kingdom was conquered by a monarch called the King of Thuc, who put Van Lang together with his own kingdom to form an empire called Au Lac. This ancient land endured for twenty-five centuries until the year 258 B.C. when the warlike Han-Chinese from the Canton area conquered Au Lac by force of arms. Vietnamese legends say that it was only through treachery within the royal family that Au Lac was defeated.

The Chinese ruled for more than a thousand years. They called the country Nam Viet and Annam (meaning "Pacification of the South"). It was a great kingdom, taking in all of today's North Vietnam and stretching into China as far as Canton. It was these people, with the mixture of others yet to come, who formed the Vietnamese peoples as they are today.

Ceremony outside temple honoring the first Emperor of Vietnam, Hung
Vuong, who lived around 1000 B.C. and had 1000 children.
(Republic of Vietnam Ministry of Information)

The new conquerors found a semicivilized series of tribes in the area. These people hunted, fished, and cultivated temporary fields, which were cleared by burning down trees. They chewed betel and had tattooed bodies. Since the victors wanted the richer coastal and river plains for themselves, they drove the natives into the hills.

The Chinese did not have an easy time in the new empire. There were repeated uprisings, some of which were temporarily successful.

In A.D. 40 two sisters, Trung Trac and Trung Nhi, led a rebellion which ousted the Chinese. For three years the former rulers were out of power, but then they returned in force and took back the land. The sisters tried to lead another uprising, but this time they were defeated and they killed themselves. Today they are considered the Indochinese counterpart of Joan of Arc, and there is a national holiday in Vietnam in their honor.

Other revolts followed, nearly all of them failures. It was not until the year 939 that the Chinese were finally driven out and Annam became a nation in its own right. Later, there were other attempts by different invaders to overcome these tough people, but in the end the Vietnamese prevailed.

Now Annam itself became an invader. It wrested the area of Saigon from the Khmers, overpowered Champa, which was then along the Vietnamese coast, and during the seventeenth and eighteenth centuries took possession of the rice-rich Mekong delta. In a proclamation of 1802 the name "Vietnam" was used for the first time, although the nation continued to be known as Annam.

By that time Europeans had discovered Indochina. Marco Polo visited Vietnam late in the thirteenth century; then came the Portuguese, the Dutch, and the English. In 1817 the French tentatively probed Vietnam and realized that the whole peninsula could be turned into a rich empire. In 1857 a French expedition took control of Annam and later on the rest of Indochina. Their rule lasted almost a century. When the French were ousted in 1954, it marked the first time in two thousand years that Indochina was free of some kind of foreign domination.

But peace did not come with freedom. Vietnam was divided in half, with the boundary line at the seventeenth parallel. Since the northern part of the country was under the influence of Communist political leaders, those people who did not wish to live under such a government were allowed to move to the southern half. Some 800,000 people, including a large number of Catholics, did migrate. Also, those in the south who wished to move north were allowed to do so.

These, then, are the Vietnamese of the Mekong delta. They are not quite like the other Indochinese in religion; Laos and Cambodia have a background of Hinduism, which, while they no longer practice it, still has had some effect on their religion. The Vietnamese are much more like the Chinese, in customs, appearance, and religion. They practice a mixture of Buddhism, Taoism, and Confucianism. Buddhism preaches compassion, self-denial, universal love for all mankind. Taoism keeps the believer in harmony with the forces of nature and the spirits. Confucianism is not really a religion; rather it is a moral code and its followers are taught to behave with respect toward parents, teachers, and elders and to truly practice the Golden Rule—"Do unto others as you would have them do unto you."

Most of the Catholics in Vietnam are in the larger cities, such as Saigon. There are not many Catholics in the delta.

According to the dictionary, a delta is a nearly flat plain of alluvial soil (the sediment of mud deposited by flowing water) between branches of a river as the river courses toward its mouth. Many times, but not always, the delta forms a rough kind of triangle. That description fits the Mekong region in South Vietnam.

As the mighty Mekong runs out of Cambodia and crosses the Vietnamese border, it begins to section itself into a number of branches, some of which are considered rivers in their own right. All these waterways, taken together, form the irregular triangle. Just thirty-five miles north of the Mekong's northern mouth (actually there are several "mouths" to the river) lies Saigon, the largest, busiest city in all of Indochina.

Vietnam's Mekong delta is perhaps the most important region in the whole peninsula, simply because it grows so much rice, sorely needed to feed the hungry millions. Many other areas look to the delta for this staple food. The delta itself is a vast cross-hatch of rivers, streams, canals, ditches, and irrigation troughs. Numerous villages and hamlets dot the heavy black clay all along the waterways and main rivers.

In a typical village the houses are made of thatch, surrounded by thickets of thorn and bamboo. Streams of busses, trucks, and other vehicles rumble through the unpaved streets. Few people in any of the villages can afford an automobile, but many have bicycles and some have motorized bikes and scooters.

The Mekong and its tributaries offer no surprises for the delta inhabitants. Floods do occur, but not often, although it is normal

Vietnamese children walk by flooded rice paddies in the Mekong Delta.
(*Wide World*)

for the land to be slightly under water during monsoon time. The Tonle Sap in Cambodia, acting as nature's storage tank, draws off the bulk of the water which would otherwise inundate the Mekong basin. Barges, sampans, junks, and other river boats make up the traffic on the main rivers. In fact, sometimes the lack of water can be a problem in the delta.

Near its mouth, where the force of the Mekong is almost spent, the various streams and canals are sometimes backed up by the encroaching sea water, which turns the soil into nonproductive land. This happens during the dry season. Also, there are some spots where there are no irrigation ditches, for it takes money to dig them and many farmers are too poor. They must rely on the small natural streams for water, and sometimes there simply isn't enough water in the stream, or it has turned bad due to sea backup.

But when the waters cover the paddies, then the farmers are out in force, standing knee-deep in the watery fields, planting the crop. Helped by a surprisingly steady climate, some years have two rice harvests. Temperatures seldom fall below 69 degrees in winter, nor rise higher than 94 degrees in summer, and are in between these two during most of the months. However, the second crop depends on how much water is available for planting. Another factor is labor. Many families do not own a buffalo to pull the plow, so they exchange labor with other families whenever possible.

The Vietnamese prize their water buffalo, which in many ways resembles a yak. These incredibly powerful creatures work tirelessly in the rice fields, wallowing contentedly in the mud, and under normal circumstances they are quite docile. The children of the farmers treat the friendly water buffalo as pets.

94

There are three dangers rice farmers must guard against if they are to bring in a good harvest. First is a tiny green-winged insect about the size of a grain of rice, called *con ray*. Second is a borer worm named *con bo*. The winged insect attacks the stems and leaves of the rice plant, while the worm bores into the stem and rots the plant. The third danger is a rust disease which turns the rice plant a brown-red color. When this disease hits the rice plant, it will not ripen.

All these dangers to the rice plants are being fought with various insecticides and disease-killers, introduced by the French and later continued by American and United Nations farm experts.

Rice is not the only crop in South Vietnam. There are numerous others: sweet potatoes, citrus fruits of all kinds, truck garden vegetables such as corn and tomatoes, and some tobacco.

In spite of the huge crops of rice and other foods, most of the farmers are poor. Their diet consists mainly of rice and a few vegetables. Even though some families may have a few pigs or chickens, and perhaps a couple of ducks swimming around the paddies, they are not eaten by the peasants. It is too costly to eat a chicken when it can be sold and the money used to buy other necessities. Beef is very rare on a farm table. Those fortunate enough to own a buffalo, which is the only source of beef, need the beast to work in the fields. Thus pork or fowl or some eggs are served on an average of twice a week, and those meals are considered feasts. During the rainy season there is fish in the streams, and families try to catch enough to eat some and salt the rest to keep for the dry months, when they become scarce again.

Another possible source of food is other kinds of animals. The

Vietnamese eat dogs, cats, rabbits, frogs, and paddy rats. On the average, a Vietnamese eats about one pound of some kind of meat or fish per week.

The peasants in the Mekong delta villages are friendly, hospitable, and superstitious. Once they realize that a stranger in their midst means them no harm, a cup of tea is offered even by the most poverty-stricken family.

In some ways, perhaps because they have come into contact with people from the West more than their neighboring countries, the Vietnamese have a somewhat modern outlook on life. For example, when a Vietnamese is sick, he will take the medicines given to him by a doctor with Western medical school training. However, just to be on the safe side, the villager will also take the herbs and potions that his ancestors took. In that way, he thinks, one of the cures will be bound to help him.

Vietnamese superstitions make use of many different kinds of animals, both real and legendary. Four creatures in particular are engraved or painted on a variety of objects in Vietnamese homes and public places: a dragon, unicorn, tortoise, and phoenix. Of these the dragon is the most important.

In Chinese and Vietnamese mythology, this beast has the head of a camel, the horns of a buck, the protruding eyes of a demon, a buffalo's ears, the neck and body of a snake, scales of a carp, claws of an eagle, and paws of a tiger. Under the creature's tongue is hidden a precious stone. It is an intelligent animal and can live in water, in air, or underground. It spits vapor that can be turned into fire at will. Dragons are immortal. Right now, according to the superstition, there aren't too many of them, but their number is increasing all the time, because there is another fabulous animal, half lizard and half snake, which can become a dragon when it has reached the age of one thousand years. A dragon may look frightening, but it is not an evil spirit. Rather it is the symbol of nobility and power, and that is why a dragon has always been identified with the old Vietnamese emperors, or "Sons of Heaven."

Most of the time village life in the delta region is peaceful. There are temples for worship, general stores where the people can buy a wide variety of articles, such as clothing, flashlights, tools, and mosquito netting. A few vendors come through the streets selling sweetmeats. But there are times—and they have occurred with increasing frequency—when the normal routine of village life is broken because of the civil strife that has engulfed this unhappy land.

The rice-rich delta region has been the scene of fighting since World War II. First the Japanese invaded, and, after they were defeated by the Allies, the Indochinese fought the French to gain independence. After those battles were done, a new conflict erupted. Large groups of people, who were called Viet Cong, wanted the Communist type of government of North Vietnam to come into power in South Vietnam. They began to wage a savage guerrilla war, not only against government troops loyal to the Saigon regime, but also against any villages whose people did not think as they did.

The people in the Mekong villages, caught in the middle, have not been permitted the luxury of neutrality. They have been forced to side with either the Viet Cong or the government troops. In the former case, rice paddy farmers will lay down their plows for a few days at a time, pick up hidden rifles, and fight alongside the guerrillas for a while, later returning to the fields to farm again. The importance of this vast, fertile basin is emphasized all the more by the realization, on both sides, that the war might well be won or lost according to which side can win out in the Mekong delta, regardless of what happens in other parts of South Vietnam.

As the slow-moving Mekong courses toward the sea, it comes almost within sight of the last and biggest of the river's cities, Saigon, often called the Pearl of the Orient.

Saigon is a city of about twenty square miles. More than two million people live, work, and play in the city's streets, alleys, and canals. It is a place of unbelievable activity. Cars, bicycles, pedicabs, horsecarts, trucks, busses, jeeps, and pedestrians swirl through the streets with no regard for traffic laws. Sampans crowd the canals, some of them serving as homes for whole families. Many other families live in shacks on stilts over the canals. There is a Saigon city law which states that houses built over water are not subject to taxes, and people take advantage of that law to save some tax money.

The Saigon seafront is constantly busy. Huge freighters, their holds bulging with cargoes of munitions, food, machinery, and clothing, lie in the harbor waiting their turn to unload. Many of the stevedores are women, since most of the men are in the army. The women can carry the heavy bags of grain almost as well as the men; they are used to doing heavy work.

The British author Rudyard Kipling, who lived in India for many years, once said, "East is East and West is West and never the twain shall meet." But he had never seen modern Saigon. A traveler need only stroll about the city's streets—where most of Saigon's life is lived—to realize in a very short time that there is no city like it anywhere in the world.

There are pretty girls, among the most beautiful to be found in any city, wearing the traditional *ao dais*, long flowing robes slit up the sides as far as the hip and worn over long trousers. The men wear Western-style sport shirts and slacks. Children are everywhere, chewing American gum or chunks of sugar cane. Soldiers crowd the streets, wearing the uniforms of their native lands—from the United States, the Philippines, Korea, and Australia, all in South Vietnam to help the cause of the Saigon government. Adding to the bustle are Buddhist worshippers on their way to their pagodas, going inside barefoot to offer gifts of fruit at the temple altars, burning red candles.

The canals seem alive with boats of all kinds. Boatmen paint eyes on the prows of their sampans, believing that they will protect them from demons.

Whatever doubts the visitor may have about the mixture of Orient and Occident are dispelled by one look at the shops and stalls that line the Saigon streets. Everywhere are displays of American canned goods, such as soups, meats, vegetables. Hanging in the butcher shops are meats and poultry, already cooked, covered with a thick red sauce, sweet and spicy. The visitor buying some of these cooked foods might be served in one of several differently decorated dishes, each of which has a different meaning. A bearded wise man painted on a plate signifies long life. A lady holding a peach indicates prosperity. A picture of a child means many descendants. A duck means good food, a deer is good luck and riches. The happiest sign of all is a red bat, for the bat sleeps with his head down and feet high. He is relaxed, with no worries at all. Or, a dish may have the ever-present dragon.

However, some of the Saigon delicacies might cause the visitor to turn away quickly, especially if he is a westerner. The people of Saigon are fond of duck heads fried in butter, or the webbed feet of a wading bird. When asked why they like such foods, the Vietnamese answer that it is not different from eating bird's nest soup, or shark fins, Chinese delicacies that are eaten by people in the United States. Probably long ago nobody ate such foods, but history has recorded many famines in the Far East. Evidently, in order to stay alive, people tried anything, even the nests of birds or the tough fins of sharks. Those fortunate enough to come upon a duck or other bird in the marshes made sure that not a drop of food was wasted.

Another mixture of East and West can be found in Saigon's entertainment. There are numerous bars, catering especially to American servicemen on furlough, and the Vietnamese have come to like such places too. Sports are popular. Soccer is the special favorite, and next comes Ping-pong. The young people of Saigon seem to be in no way different from American teen-agers. They think rock and roll music is absolutely the greatest, and have adopted all the Western types of dancing.

Saigon is not a clean city. There are great problems with sanitation, for the city was never intended to hold so many people. In the last twenty years the population has almost doubled. And, as more and more industry comes into Saigon, the problems increase. Today there are flour and rice mills in the city, factories producing commercial alcohol, molasses, cooking oil, and fish sauce. On the seacoast itself are plants that produce salt by distilling sea water. There is little provision for waste materials. All the residue of living and commerce is dumped into the canals as untreated sewage, and often it seeps into the drinking pipes. Even in hospitals there is little or no plumbing.

United States doctors and sanitary engineers are trying desperately to correct this situation, but it is a long and difficult task. Perhaps when the war is over and there is time for peaceful work, Saigon can become a clean city again.

Now, as the Mekong and its tributaries leave the delta land of South Vietnam, its hamlets, villages, and cities, its journey is done. The great river that was born 2,600 miles away in the towering Himalaya Mountains of the Kham region in Tibet swirls the final few miles and dies, giving up its brown salt-filled waters to the South China Sea.

CHAPTER 7

The Future of the Mekong

In June of 1965 two fast jet boats, presented to the United Nations by the government of New Zealand, succeeded in navigating the treacherous, rapid-filled Khone Falls, which lie on the Laos-Cambodian border of the Mekong River. That was the first time in history that boats of any kind succeeded in moving through this area under their own power.

In March of 1966 a power project was completed in northeast Thailand. It was constructed along the Nam Pong River, whose waters flow into the Mekong.

These examples are among the first steps taken by the United Nations to harness the full power of the mighty Mekong.

In 1951 the UN established the Economic Commission for Asia and the Far East—nicknamed ECAFE. Its purpose was to investigate the possible development of the Mekong River resources. The

Jet-powered survey boat on the Mekong. (*United Nations*)

people of Laos, Thailand, Cambodia, and Vietnam were in dire need of help. In Thailand, for example, which has always been the most advanced Mekong country, the average peasant earned less than $100 per year. There were 54 million people in those countries, and half of them lived in the lower Mekong region. By the end of the twentieth century there would probably be about 90 million people in the same area. Without some sort of planning for the future, there was great danger of mass starvation.

A team of seven experts made surveys and returned with an enthusiastic report which they called "the dream document." It contained plans for projects that would help in irrigation, flood control, navigation, and electric power. They pointed out that the lower Mekong, from the top of Laos to the mouth of the river at the South China Sea, ran for some 1,500 miles, making it just as long as the Mississippi River.

Villagers gather around a Canadian survey plane on the Mekong in Thailand. *(United Nations)*

As to what all the series of dams and power stations might mean to the Mekong peoples:

In time it might be possible to take a boat from the South China Sea all the way up to Luang Prabang, a distance of 1,000 miles.

Floods would be a danger of the past. The Tonle Sap would still get some backup water to fill its lake region, but not as much. Other sections in Laos, Cambodia, and Vietnam would never have to worry again about flooding.

Irrigation with a dependable water supply could make two rice crops a year a certainty. Thus there would be a greater food supply for Indochina's hungry millions.

The various power stations would do for Indochina what the Tennessee Valley Authority did for some states in the U.S.A.— furnish cheap electric power, which could be fed by cables to communities far away—even into North Vietnam. This in turn would mean the establishment of industries in the Mekong countries. The generators, fed by the surging waters of the Mekong, could electrify the entire peninsula. The jungles could be pushed back, making more of the land open for farming.

The idea of developing the Mekong River resources was received with enthusiasm by the UN, but, at the same time, the member nations realized that there would be many problems. First was money. The whole series of dams, reservoirs, power stations and the endless miles of cable, the relay points, and generators would cost about 3 billion 300 million dollars. Then there was the problem of mainland China. Suppose that government, which is not a member of the UN, decided to divert that part of the Mekong which flowed through its country? Also, the four Mekong nations had a long history of boundary disputes.

Several of these problems have already been settled. An agreement has been reached by twenty-one countries, in addition to the Mekong nations, to pay the necessary money over a period of ten years. River experts have pointed out that even if China did divert its portion of the Mekong, that would only take away one third of the river's water, and there would still be plenty left for all the projects. Besides, if mainland China did divert the Mekong, it would have to channel the new course into the Salween River, and that might cause serious flooding in southern Yünnan. Therefore, it would probably never be done.

So, a start has been made. Hopefully, in the not-too-distant future all the Mekong projects will be completed. The peoples of the Indochinese peninsula will reap the rewards and riches that can be theirs in the harnessing of the mighty Mekong. They and their children will have a better way of life. And all the fighting will have ceased!

The United Nations has called the mighty Mekong "a sleeping giant." Some day, very soon, the sleeping giant of Indochina will awaken!

Bibliography

BUTTINGER, JOSEPH. *The Smaller Dragon.* New York: Frederick A. Praeger.

CARRASCO, PEDRO. *The Land and Polity in Tibet.* American Ethnological Society.

CHI JEN CHANG. *The Minority Groups of Yunnan.* Ann Arbor, Michigan: University of Michigan.

DE BERVAL, RENÉ. *The Kingdom of Laos.* Limoges: A. Bontemps Co. Ltd.

DO VANG LI. *Aggression by China.* Delhi: Siddhartha Publications Ltd.

FIFIELD, RUSSELL H., and SCHAFF, C. HART. *The Lower Mekong.* Princeton, New Jersey: Van Nostrand.

FUSON, C. G. *The New Geography of China.* Commercial Press Ltd., Shanghai.

HENDRY, JAMES B., and VAN-THUAN, NGUYEN. *The Study of a Vietnamese Rural Community.* East Lansing, Michigan: Michigan University Viet Nam Advisory Group.

LE BAR, FRANK, ed., and STAFF OF THE HUMAN RELATIONS AREA FILES. *Laos, Its People, Society, Culture.* Human Relations Area Files Press. New York: Taplinger.

LITTLE, ARCHIBALD. *The Far East*. New York: Clarendon Press.

PEREIRA, GENERAL GEORGE. *Peking to Lhasa*. Constable Press.

STEINBERG, DAVID J., and others. Staff of the Human Relations Area Files. *Cambodia, Its People, Society, Culture*. Human Relations Area Files Press. New York: Taplinger.

THOMPSON, P. A. SIAM. J. B. Millet Co.

TRAN VAN TUNG. *Vietnam*. New York: Thames & Hudson.

WARD, CAPTAIN F. KINGDON. *The Mystery Rivers of Tibet*. London: Seely Service & Co. Ltd.

WEST CHINA UNION UNIVERSITY MUSEUM GUIDEBOOK SERIES. *An Introduction to Tibetan Culture*. Chengtu, China.

Index

Allies, 49, 97
Amithaba, 27
Angkor Thom, Cambodia, 75, 80
Angkor Wat, Cambodia, 75
Animals, 14, 20, 22, 28, 30, 32, 48, 52,
    54, 65–66, 69, 78, 94, 95–96. *See also
    separate listings*
Annam, 54, 88–91
Ao dais, 99
Asia (Asian), 13, 14, 17, 18, 26, 53
Au Lac, 88
Australia, 99

Bamboo, 63
Bassac River, 83
Bayon, 75
Boats, 14, 56, 78, 80, 94, 98, 99, 102.
    See also separate listings
Brahmaputra River, 13, 18
Bridges, 23, 24, 49

Buddha (Buddhism), 25–26, 37, 54,
    56–59, 80, 81, 82, 91, 99
Buffalo, water, 94
Burma, 13, 14, 39, 44, 48–51, 54, 56
Burma Road, 48

Cambodia (Cambodian), 16, 17, 53,
    54, 63, 73, 74–87, 91, 92, 102–06
Camels, 28
Caravans, 24
Catholics, 91, 92
Chamdo, Tibet, 24–25, 36
Champa tribe, 53, 90
Cham tribe, 74
Ch'angtu. *See* Chamdo
Chao Phraya River, 56, 62
Chin tribe, 45
China (Chinese), 13, 14, 20, 24, 26,
    30, 34, 36, 37–48, 50, 53, 62, 81, 88–
    90, 91, 96, 100, 105

Chu-ba, 32
Chung ts'ao, 35–36
Commerce. *See* Merchants
Confucianism, 91
Crops. *See* Farms
Customs: Cambodian, 82, 83; Laotian, 61, 64–66; Lolo, 41–44; Tibetan, 28–31; Vietnamese, 96, 99–100

Dalai Lama, 20
Delta, Mekong River, 17, 87, 88–101
De Rhins, Detreuil, 18–19
Dien Bien Phu, 54
Dokerla Pass, 37
Dutch, 75, 91
Dzachu River. *See* Nam Chu River

East China Sea, 50
Economic Commission for Asia and the Far East (ECAFE), 102–06
English. *See* Great Britain
Europeans. *See separate listings*

Fa Ngum, 59
Farms: Cambodian, 76, 78, 87; Chinese, 48; Laotian, 61; Tibetan, 32–34; Vietnamese, 94–96, 97–98
Fish (fishing), 16, 62–63, 65, 81, 84–87, 95
Flower Feast, 26
Food, 30–31, 35, 87, 92, 95–96, 99–100
Forests, 23, 63, 76
Fortunetellers. *See* Superstitions
France (French), 18–19, 54, 63, 75, 76, 91, 95, 97
Funanese, 74

Glaciers, 18
Gomba, 22
Great Britain (British), 19, 30, 41, 91
Great International River, the, 13

Han-Chinese, 88

Hau Giang River, 17
Headhunters, 45
Herbs. *See* Medicine
Herdsmen, 28–32
Himalaya Mountains, 13, 18, 34, 49, 101
Hindu, 26, 74, 75, 82, 91
Houses, 30, 76–78, 86–87, 98

India, 18, 25, 34, 35, 39, 49, 74, 98
Indians, American, 36, 45–48
Indochina (Indochinese), 53, 54, 56, 74, 80, 81, 82, 90, 91, 97, 104, 105, 106
Industry, 105; Laotian, 64; Vietnamese, 100–01
Irrawaddy River, 13, 41
Irrigation, 17, 34, 94, 103, 104

Japanese, 49, 97
Joan of Arc, 90
Junks, 78, 80, 94
Jyekundo, Tibet, 24

Kachin tribe, 45
Kha tribe, 53
Kham region, Tibet, 18, 24–25, 31, 38, 48, 101
Khmer Lake, 64
Khmer tribe, 53, 59, 73, 74–75, 80, 90
Khone Falls, 16, 73, 102
Khong, Laos, 73
Khun Borom, 52–53
Khun Lo, 53–54
Kipling, Rudyard, 98
Korea, 99
Kratie, Cambodia, 76
Kublai Khan, 39–41, 48–49, 50, 54
Kunming, Yünnan, 49

Lamaism, 26
Lamas, 19, 26
Lamaseries, 25, 26, 34–35

Lants'ang Kiang, 13, 38
Lan-Xang, 53–54, 69–70
Laos (Laotian), 14, 16, 50, 52–73, 74, 78, 83, 91, 102–06
Lashio, Burma, 49
Ledo, India, 49
Ledo Road, 48
Legends: Laotian, 52–53, 62; Tibetan, 27–28; Vietnamese, 88
Lhasa, Tibet, 24
Likiang-Nashi tribe, 36
Lolo tribe, 41–44
Luang Prabang, Laos, 14, 56, 70, 78, 104
Lumbering. *See* Forests

Malaria, 23, 38
Manushin Buddha, 27
Martaban, Gulf of, 50
Medicine, 24, 35–36, 69, 101
Menam River, 62
Meo tribe, 66
Merchants, 24, 31, 56, 70, 75, 81, 96, 99
Miao tribe, 48
Minerals, 35, 48, 69
Mining, 35, 48
Mongols, 39–41
Monsoon, 16, 34, 48, 50, 61–62, 66, 70, 76, 84, 94
Moslems, 39

Naga tribe, 45
Nam Chu River, 13, 38
Nam Pong River, 102
Nam Seng River, 16
Nam Viet, 88
Nang-Chen tribe, 34
Nashi tribe, 45
New Zealand, 102
Nirvana, 61
Norodom Sihanouk, Prince, 76
Nuoc nam sauce, 87

Nu Shan Mountains, 18

Pa boeuk fish, 62
Padek fish, 63
Padmasambhava, 25–26
Pagan, Burma, 50
Pagoda, 56, 65, 70, 78, 99
Pak Lay, Laos, 66
Panchen Lama, 20
Paoshan, Yünnan, 50
Phi, 59
Philippines, 99
Phnom Penh, Cambodia, 16, 63, 76, 78–82, 83, 87
Phra Bang, 59
Pirogues, 14, 56, 78
Po, 27
Polo, Marco, 50, 90
Portugal (Portuguese), 75, 90–91
Pradith, Khamchan, 64
P'u tribe, 41

Quatres Bras, 83

Religion. *See separate listings*
Rice, 17, 61, 69, 76, 78, 87, 92, 94, 95, 104
Rubber growing, 76

Saigon, South Vietnam, 63, 90, 92, 98–101
Salween River, 13, 14, 18, 23, 37, 41, 48–49, 50, 105
Sampans, 14, 56, 78, 80, 94, 99
Sampots, 81
Sanskrit, 35
Savang Vanthana, King, 52
Savannakhet, Laos, 16
School, 34–35
Se Noi River, 16
Shan tribe, 45
Ships. *See* Boats
Siam. *See* Thailand

Sikang province, 14, 38, 41, 48, 50
Siva, 75
Slingshot, 32
South China Sea, 17, 87, 101, 103, 104
Sports, 82, 100
Stilwell Road, 48
Superstitions: Cambodian, 81–83; Laotian, 59–61, 69; Thai, 67–69; Tibetan, 26–27; Vietnamese, 96
Switzerland, 38

Takang, 87
Tangin Pass, Tibet, 13, 19
Taoism, 91
Tennessee Valley Authority, 104
Thailand (Thai), 14, 16, 39, 52, 53–56, 63, 66–73, 74, 75, 80, 102–06
Thanglha Mountains, 19
Thuc, king of, 88
Tibet, 13, 18–36, 37, 41, 44, 48, 50, 62, 101
Tibetan-Shan plateau, 38
Tonle Sap Lake, 16, 76, 84–87, 94, 104
Tonle Sap River, 16, 76, 83, 84–87
Trading. See Merchants
Transportation, 92, 98
Trey reach fish, 87
Trung trei, 86

Turbulent river, the, 13, 38

United Nations, 95, 102–06
United States (American), 36, 49, 95, 99, 100, 101, 104

Van Lang, 88
Vientiane, Laos, 16, 56, 69–73
Viet Cong, 97
Vietnam, North, 54, 88, 105
Vietnam, South, 17, 54, 63, 88–101, 103–06

Wa tribe, 45, 51
War, Vietnamese, 97–98, 99, 106
Ward, Frank Kingdon, 19, 41
Water Feast, 26
Wat Phnom, Cambodia, 80
World War II, 48–50, 75, 97
Wuman tribe, 41

Yaks, 20, 28, 30–31, 94
Yangtze River, 13, 14, 18, 23, 50, 53
Yao tribe, 45, 46
Yellow River, 13
Yungling Shan Mountains, 18
Yünnan, 14, 37–48, 49, 50, 105
Yushu. See Jyekundo